DREAMING IN THE BONE BOAT

Dreaming in the Bone Boat: Poems
Copyright © 2022 by Raymond "Moose" Jackson.
All rights reserved.
ISBN: 978-1-60801-233-6

Cover photograph: Brian Zeigler
Cover and book design by Alex Dimeff.

Printed in the United States of America on
acid-free paper.

UNIVERSITY OF NEW ORLEANS PRESS
2000 Lakeshore Drive
New Orleans, Louisiana 70148
unopress.org

DREAMING
IN THE BONE BOAT

poems

raymond "moose" jackson

UNIVERSITY OF NEW ORLEANS PRESS

CONTENTS

INTRODUCTION
13

channeled inspiration
17

close as the moon can come
18

vacuus viator
19

morpheus aux barricades
21

heaven is a subtle thing
23

hide your eyes
24

i know where you got them shoes
25

riverbent
26

getting shabby at the abbey
27

invite the flood
28

an end to vicious rumours
30

anxious sound
32

envie
34

good omen
36

river watch
37

a love unsinkable
38

seawolf dejá vu
39

secret nowhere garden
40

the apple will catch
41

a dream of black wolves
43

spiders are writers
44

the boy at the smokehouse door
45

the coronation
46

maison poulet
50

the prosthetic miracles of st. roch
51

coyote and white crane
53

lunch with the baroness de pontalba
55

regain the silence
56

secondline
58

sobriety's anxieties
60

takes a dummy to know
61

the mule trade
63

wolfsbane
64

home after the missed disaster
66

living the cliché
68

hometown haints
69

we got this day
71

thrown bones
73

the holy boat
74

the knickerbocker
75

dreaming in the bone boat
78

the night of entwined dragons
79

gnash
81

the way through
83

in towns where they still
know each other
84

slipping the perfect gig-line
86

the punctual
88

the man in the black hat
89

now start again
90

fly on home
91

rootfire
93

isleño lullaby
94

presence in the strike
96

the shining vision
97

the gardener's prayer
98

the ceremony of night
100

the danger angels
102

the will to change
103

halo
104

community agriculture
105

mardi gras raven
106

dancing to the gates
108

rebuilding
110

the suchness of migration
111

i want to make love to you
112

flood street
115

whippoorwill
116

sugarskull complicity
117

the cone of probability
119

the downshift
121

the ego hunters
122

raccoon sarcasm
123

the beautiful bones
125

summertime lull
126

smoking monk
127

the bear witness
128

recordkeepers
129

the power of music
131

breaking and entering
133

INTRODUCTION

One part of poetry is for me a holy mnemonic.
I have been a pilgrim my whole life and what
I record is just a glimmer of the ongoing
conversation that I am having with the divine
self as we walk the path. These are some of my
footsteps: I was born in Detroit, my mother's and
father's lines are a mix of Swiss-German, Scotch-
Irish, Shawnee and on both sides, Cherokee. My
dad was a factory worker, my mom a waitress.
I joined the military out of high school. The
Air Force trained me to be a Spanish Language
crypto-analyst. Military service did not train
out my sense of duty to all people, especially
the poor, nor did it stunt my compassion. I
learned things in my work that I was morally
traumatized by. I cross-trained and became
an aeromedical technician, but by that time
the moral imperative to follow higher orders
had seized me, and I soon left the service. I
explored the possibility of joining the catholic
priesthood. I went to live in the pilgrimage
town of Santiago de Compostela, in Spain. When
I returned to the states I worked for a year
as professional theater actor then began my
own intelligence-gathering pilgrimage through
America's underbelly by hopping freight trains,
squatting and hitch-hiking. I got into punk
rock and direct action. During those voyages I
became frustrated with the laundry list format
of my journaling, and turned to poetry as a
sort of compressed data means of recording my
experiences and expanding perception. Each one

is a code, a spell, a zip file for myself to unpack a host of memories and milestones.

REALIZATIONS

Travelling like that was a mystical experience, especially since I opened myself to the spiritual aspect of poetry. But magic can turn tragic, too. I realized it was time to, in the words of Gary Snyder, "get intimate with a watershed". I needed the connection and accountability of a community. I had spent the coldest winter in 50 years in a unfinished shack in Cap Breton, Nova Scotia. My dreams sang of soft southern winds. I hopped freight trains and hitch-hiked down to New Orleans in 2003 and learned to dance with disaster.

Living in New Orleans for the past few decades has scored and sculpted my perception. The magical is real, the profane; sacred. The living share houses and streets with the dead. All my friends are cosmic psychonaut journeymen, leaving this world hootin' and hollerin' and headed for the stars. I live and breathe a totemic animism in these streets and cemeteries, in parades and in the wild-yowling night. These poems are documentation of the spirit walk that is our collective pilgrimage.

Some of these poems can be read as invocation of the reality we wish to build: prayers, calls for help, remembrance and release of our pain. They have been shared as theater and music and carnival culture. We know how to ritualize important passages in this place. We perform ceremony together in the streets. Our culture celebrates our transformations, our initiations and our losses. The past two years have limited our ability to gather, but it has not stopped us from working through our collective loss. And we lose a lot here, whether by storm or crime or erosion or gentrification. We are learning how to release. We learn how important it is to remember spirit, and to live for today. When others despair, we dance.

r. moose jackson
03jan22, new orleans

CHANNELED INSPIRATION

we got so little ground to stand on
we have not fed the ancestors
we have not kept the seasons
we dance just to keep the spirits quiet
but they won't stay down long

see them spinning off the fingers
of musicians, squishing out of
tubes of paint, mad scribbling in a haste
flinging bodies about the room

there are moments when we fly
some of that is us; showing up
but a lot of it is spirits
borrowing our craft
savouring our struggle
to express universal truth

the time left to us is short
we are down to the final pages
so let us speak directly

it's really not about us
except in the way that we are vital
links in a very long chain

the end feels like it's close
let's dance the night away

CLOSE AS THE MOON CAN COME

hold this even unto the bone:
                    that night!
you jostled a thundergod
riding in a borrowed plastic bathtub
under a full press of sail
how she rolled for you, and your mad mates
like a dolphin offering his soft undersides

you review your life and know
that you've been a drunkard and a rake
but now it's salt and wet and the moon is full
now you are true
now you are human
and your small craft is under advisory
because nature cannot be predicted
and anyway
here is where you are, just now

could be disaster.
doesn't matter
you find your slot
and you surf

VACUUS VIATOR

there are dark passes
that the soul must push through

there are storm-pressed paths
treacherous switchbacks
near-death experiences
      to render raw the heart
      to break pride and dependence

only the empty-handed are ever free:
there are visions and visitations
well-worn maps and silent ravens
early-morning meditations and
midnight moonlight ministrations
of love along the roadside
to soothe the wilder archetypes

there's the looming spectacle of death
on the highway, in the city streets
at the end of a needle: altered states
to impregnate the timeline with meaning

there are visions which come to fruition
when you only thought that you were dreaming

so do not quit this life, despite
all disappointments, all pain, all strife
do not go to sleep before the night
but remain; until the end
of the last refrain
the last note of the last song
til only its absence lays
shimmering in the dusky air

so you can at last turn to yourself and say
"i was there."
knowing we danced through every darkness
loved without guarantee
and when you go, go empty-handed
the better to know that you are free

MORPHEUS AUX BARRICADES

maybe it's the proximity of battlefields
that has denied me these nights of dreaming
morpheus cross-armed at the gates
withholding his slumbering mercies

at root i am a soldier
i have marching orders to outlast the battle
sitting sentry on the motel floor
while my animal runs down the song lines

it isn't your ricefield
that the gods have been targeting
but you still wake up shell-shocked
beat to hell for harboring this refugee

> nobody asked for this calamity.
> we don't even know the parties
> that are at war.

i've often wondered if we're defective
designed twain, yet composite
and saddled with a penchant for friendly fire

those two spots on the yin and yang
one light and one dark:
                bullet holes.
it is a cycle of mutual piercing

they say it's bad luck to question the
        engineering
but i've had to live with the defects
all my hard-knock life
and i've a few suggestions for your comments
        box

duck and cover
under the covers
or sit ramrod still all night
                    just breathing
they can't keep you out of the dream palace
    forever

wars do come to an end
one way or another

when the old man comes trundling by
unawares,
i'm gonna jump up out the ground
i'm gonna get some answers
for the nights that i spent on watch

HEAVEN IS A SUBTLE THING

the colours are brighter than i remember
a temper in the air
of tolerance, awareness
it is no longer a chore
to rise into the form of a focusing buddha

we are witnessing the death of science fiction:
everything we never believed in
is bearing itself into our unprepared hands

i am trying to recall
what i read in the crumbling text
about the transition to shambhala
re-entry into the realm of gods
how you know you've woken under a bench
in the mead hall of valhalla

heaven, i think
is a subtle thing
as much a quality of light
as any lightness of being

verily, verily
it exists within ye

a calling wildness
a brighter colour
sneaks up on you
just when you've embraced your spare existence

HIDE YOUR EYES
summer 2005

everyone so shy.
hide your eyes because
it's not yet your hour
              to shine

keep it private from the rest
this is for the family
which we only recognize
by bike frames and patches
                  on our vests
freak tags and hopeful stares
at the corner store
in the middle of the night

the outside world
could never see us right
so we gather seated, on cold floors
open our doors
circled round this desperate guitarist

and how many tribes
don't even have this?
i could easily cry
for the emptiness of america

which is maybe why we hide our eyes
because if we opened up
and looked around
the tears would flood
the streets would drown

I KNOW WHERE YOU GOT THEM SHOES

yeah, it's my own fault
i been on a two-day bender
seventeen days into lent

i lost my shoes in jackson square
i know; i'm drunk. worse than that
leaning with intent to fall
you know what they say:
if you can't make it in new orleans...
                    don't leave.

i started asking people if they might
have an extra pair
that would fit me

fifty-seven people later
somebody gave me the shoes off their feet

yeah you right.
the town's a pain in the ass
can rip you down, rob you blind
but there ain't no bottom
to her kindness for folk like us:
gutterpunks, drunks
homebums and crackheads
she proudly employs wingnut queens
junkies and buskers
and all old-school hustlers
and the rest of us
kar-ack-teurs
down here still
livin' the dream

RIVERBENT

wasn't it this bend of the river
where you tried to map out our delta?
destiny forking in contrary visions
while the water wandered balefully by

downriver from our voiced convictions
the natives report that we are still dancing
gathering the silted waters
to hang above the heads of the rich

if there could be a job for us
it would be this
the confluence of our conflict spent
in spellwork undoing our duties

but our country can't stand us
to be out of their sight
already the phone is ringing
and we will have to put destiny on hold
as you climb into the truck
and go back to work

GETTING SHABBY AT THE ABBEY

how ancient are these tavern tables?
banded by steel and bound by memories
of lives leaking melodies and liquid spirit
raptured nights of ruptured dreams
lacquered in the layers of the laymen's histories
we can lament the loss if they close the gates
but hell stays open through
hurricanes and heartbreaks

long after we sober up, grow up, and move on
the tables might be turned
but they will remain, unless
it all goes below again

and if that happens
what are we gonna have left to hold onto?
lifesavers, neighbors, rescue boats and ropes
our hope's in stasis
in the stained-glass ceiling
a frozen disco ball
the pictures on the wall
the abbey's filled with the wreckage
of devastated decades, dedicated
to our devil-may-care demise
the smoke rolls by in waves

you have grown some roots, perchance
        i have birthed some scars:

the river
remembers nothing

INVITE THE FLOOD

i don't mind the water coming in
under the door
through the vent in the ceiling
god's been on a creative streak
visiting us in our dreams
making appearances in latté foam
roaming the ragged edges of our world
thinking about recycling

actually, i invite it in
especially if it comes in
with your hair and skin
the regular breathing of this dog
                sweetgrass
a typewriter on the door-for-a-desk
and a rainy dawn through the windows of the
    caravan

that sings and risks
the roar of golden disks paired
with oscilloscope obelisks
in the abandoned church and a fellow pilgrim
to sink down with me
in profound meditation

when i give you these poems
still wet from inundation
it is because i love you
i could tear a hole in my chest
and let it flood the city streets

the reason i'm so busy carving this soul
is to make of it a gift
to be strong in vulnerability
to be one with the weather and its cycles
and you, and our people
living loving fighting dying
to be free

AN END TO VICIOUS RUMOURS

the truth was bound to come out:
that we are finding the temper of our mettle
in this pressure cooker for the soul
a phoenix fire, turned up hot
on our metaphysical pot of gumbo

the work is here, and i'm about
the task at hand: the buzz
from our busy streets
winding through these metaphors
metamorphosis, the chrysalis
death card
endings-come-beginnings
endurance

but i can't claim we are re-building
for nothing remains the same
and there is no insurance policy against
the lurking disaster of change

and we couldn't save ourselves
even if we tried
and i have tried / almost died
all this imagery of water keeps
washing my sandcastles out to sea

the penguin and the walrus have said goodnight
shake the hankie, blow the tuba
another boatload of what we had left to hold onto
is pulling away from the burning wharf
while those of us who still remain
are gaining an awareness
of just how deep
and dark the forest may be

whoever it is, playing with the lights
and pulling on our strings
has given up on trying to make us dance
and has turned to a life of shadowpuppets
to re-animate his nights

some folks say the city by the bay
is poised for its imminent demise
but we carry our faultlines in our hearts
so it's no surprise to us
that today we got delirious tremors

we come to understand, by and by
that it's not the alligator's job to say
"beware the alligators"
so drink a little poison 'fore ye die
and dance like this bywater slowjam
is truly the last of its kind

kali's presence in this place
brings me to my knees daily
truly, thanks to y'all and the *baron samedi*
i now know piety like the psalms of my hands

i was chastised yesterday
for questioning nature, human and otherwise
but i'd still like to know:
by what charm
is the minotaur dragging the virgin
back to her chains
behind the seat of cassiopeia?

and i wonder what strange voodoo's gonna
        break loose
from this water-phoenix chrysalis
when we bed down our vicious rumours

ANXIOUS SOUND
allways lounge

you just stand there
eyes closed
tapping on that saxophone
i know you're hearing ghosts
i'm hearing them, too
they're always here
skitter-swirling about this room

town is flooded with their animal funk
every wingnut babe and buck
come here from the countries of the
dispossessed
step in it, sooner or later
then make of themselves a nuisance
trying to get in the act

not really their fault, i guess
they ain't real enough
to drive their own vehicles
enough, i guess; that the blood still gushes
enough, i said; this music
is enough to go crazy to
and it's crazy, too

it's the dead dregs of new orleans summer
jobless dread and going for broke
these ghosts don't care we're playing for
peanuts
they don't care that we're here
but i still hear them
their song, when it's lucid
goes back to the riots, the war, prohibition
acquisition

they are still here
we always hear
their gentle, mad resolution

ENVIE

the cool white
hexagonal tiles
wood panels and fans ornate
mirrors and marble, tall windows
the wide expanse of french doors open
to the quarter suggests
a café in france
would make you think
that we are elegant, and well-heeled
bohemian brats but it's all a ruse
southern gothic subterfuge

this den of slightly demonic drunks
the drug-users and history buffs
shams and losers
we are the back-of-house misanthropes
bartenders who get too loose on Toulouse
drifters and grifters
banjo buskers, old-school hustlers
and erudite burlesque queens
we may rule the night on this street
but by day, we beat the heat
with espresso over ice

you came here to loaf, maybe write
(by 3 the place is lousy with poets)
the baristas have class, tempered by sass
they still allow dogs but no smoking;
that's a thing of the past

of course, the tables outside are perfect for that
it's a perfect little addiction, indeed
almost a need, a habit as much as habitat
so stop
and admire all this wild *life*
at café envie
where passions are freed

GOOD OMEN

there are signs i take for good luck
rain at a funeral
wine we've spilt in our toast
the numerology of good fortune
when it lies in infinite repose

not so much luck, i suppose
as confirmation that we're on the right path.

when numbers lend themselves to sacred poetry
and words align with celestial math
we put all the money we had on this:

                2, for a win.

longshot romantics hooked on the gambol
with mercury in retrograde
coyote howled and grinned
we took our chances and
        look how it paid!

RIVER WATCH

rusted red, the eternal tanker
slanks into view, riding high
upriver bound, low whistle blows
the steamer's paddle plunging
churning and pulsing

south wind is blowing up from the gulf
smelling of marsh and cypress seed
the river's been low: the sand bar below
is full of weeds and small trees

another tanker, black and low
swings dangerous down
on its way back to sea

and i'm stuck here.
on the river's edge
wishing i had a sailor's life
sea my home, sea my wife
at night dreaming on the foam
about the trip to heaven's shore

a dark cloud reaches out from the west bank
where the current runs faster
a carving disaster
threatens to spill, run wild
down the delta of my dreaming

A LOVE UNSINKABLE

under the veneer of normalcy
there is a knowledge
that these are the dying breaths of a legend

and we say we're here to stay
but everyone is readying the lifeboats

i wipe a frightful tear from your cheek;
you find it hard to believe
that this is terra firma

the upshot of running with nomadic capricorns
is that this
is about as stable as it gets:
we are always seeking higher ground

with the memory of elephants
i have moved into the ark
thinking upon next year's flood

in more desperate times
we're allotted berths in twos
which has secured you passage
in a love that is unsinkable

when the relief cheques have blown away
and the last trumpet note drifts across the river
we will then take to the sea
and find our home in one another

SEAWOLF DEJÁ VU

was that really us out there?
scoring over silvered swells
our viking blood emboldened by
the moon ablaze in a southern gale

and the gloom behind the headsail
betrayed me
portrayed me
older than this one life could allow

was that not our night raid?
like others from before this ride
two seawolves on the turning tide
laughing into the darkness

would you recognize those eyes
if you'd met them
when we were both dragons?
stretched upon the moon-glazed sound
did we go into battle together?
were we leaders in forces of darkness?

here we have met
as pirate punk sailors
open-heart giants
on courageous seas of compassion

love booms out across the waves
the torn sail is singing its ruin, and rebirth
formidable in its transitional aspect

SECRET NOWHERE GARDEN

within the walls
of my secret nowhere garden
i hear stories of castle squats
gypsy reunions on mexican beaches
and the everpresent sirens of doom

the world's a-swirl with beauty and danger
unending possibilities
of nightmare and paradise
co-creating this one
confounded plane

and i'm brought to task
back at the center
of my middle road reality

by black tea, in a green earth mug
blue dog scratching at his fleas
a baby crow beseeching
growing, preparing to learn
gathering sacred memories
with the foresight of high flyers

the garden is the center
from which springs
the ten thousand things

the jimmy-rigged junk
and the sprouting beans
all sing with the voice of eternity, here

THE APPLE WILL CATCH

i did not so much mind
standing with you, in that broken place
cold and dark in puddles.
the rain coming in.

wicked dwarves made vicious entrances
entranced us with their gleeful,
awful sin
we hid amongst the stumps
and you shared your poison apple

the symbolism is not lost on me:
our inner states keep being reflected
through the scrappy arts of our punk relations
and we fit so well in that fantasy forest
two dark elves, wistful and weird
then whisked away before any other creatures
could pierce our elusive mystique

for we prefer mystery to mastery
doomed dreams and dramatic escapes
i tell you to sit with your deadly sin
and i will sit with mine, but
you dance with grasping
i dance with aversion

can these abuses still be called love?
across town, authentic self
is waiting in the rain
for dwarves and elves to take their bows
and pardon us our iniquities

gluttony, envy
wrath,
and sloth
have gone to work on the mind machine
they are going to pull an all-nighter

while greed, pride, and
lust-in-the-kitchen
are baking pies with
the scarlet witch of business

we know this story too well
they are going to wreck it all
to show us the emptiness
of our ramshackle glory
this lovely mess
our romantic ruin

then the sun will come out
and someone will demand the rent

that apple
will catch in our throats

A DREAM OF BLACK WOLVES

the moon rose on bighorn mountain
solemn through the trees
the fire was banked and dying down
and i lay beside my love to sleep

and in my sleep i was dreaming
that i was back outside again
and i spied wolves upon the ridge
who set to howling
and i howled, too
and then a few brave ones joined
close to me
just beyond the firelight
young wolves, black wolves
eyes feral and calm and penetrating

one by one
they leaped for my throat
i held my ground: remained empty
returned their noble stares
with respect and a wordless knowing
as young wolves sailed
past me in the moonlight

SPIDERS ARE WRITERS

there are spiders
everywhere tonight
grandma spiders and trickster spiders
and spiders padding their own egg sacs

                    soon to be airborne
                    on silk sailing ships

there are spiders dripping from poets' chins
                    and pork pie brims

you've got to get past the inhibitions
of eight articulated hairy legs
and eyeballs, black
                unblinking
the twisting language of DNA strands
                indra's net
whole galaxies caught in the dew drops

spiders know a lot of secrets
slip a silver coin in the slot
and whisper to the egrets
i remind you, lest you forget:

i read the spider's alphabet

THE BOY AT THE SMOKEHOUSE DOOR

they call on you
in the middle of the night
to build the fire; to feed it
the blood of trees
those upright denizens
breathe the smoke as an offering

the reason why is the hogs
soaking in the blood and the brine
i saw them laid out on metal trays
i saw them stacked on smokehouse rack
they look an awful lot
                    like us.

feel the human weight of them
touch their teeth. touch a dead eye
these too, were our people

look, i'll serve you
some whiskey and brisket, but
don't ask me to talk about it

i'm busy asking the universe why
we gotta kill to live. all this business
the successful entrepreneurs
the technocrat class

we'll meet here at the blackened bar
to take in the smoke and spin old vinyl
watch the traffic dwindle
and consider the sacrifice

compassionate butchers that we are

THE CORONATION
ash wednesday 2015

1.
this would not be
the first time i tried
to describe the arc of this alchemy

one thing i know:
a thing has to be able to die
in order to truly live

i don't remember who it was
sitting at the fire pit
talking about mayan sacrifices
but when that stranger fell to earth
the witches on the roofline went silent
and i knew the night was over

so ended the first cycle;
loss

2.
back into the womb-room
rune-wound
for another transformation
chasing the dawn awash
in the detritus we'd gathered from flood

what exactly was the parable of our quagmire?
you have to be able to take your hope and hatred
and hold them in the same hand
and honestly see them as one
and this will make you a better people

follow this up with service
to your fellow beings
sweep the floors
take out their trash
sleep is for those who have finished their work
we all sleep in the end
but some of us burn long tapers
sitting vigil on the inner darkness
so ends the second cycle;
purification

3.
the next day went to the wolves
lean and agile in their intuitions
tactical in their ritual
even their play had an element of danger

right relation is relevant
the water will keep you close to duty
imbalance brings a duppy armed
with a volley of angry rocks

the normals have their
prognostic proclamations
predictive predilection
parameters

i don't claim to have
jesus on the mainline
but we beat their fearsome odds
and made harbor at the flash of the storm
thus completing the cycle of re-wilding

4.

on tuesday morning
we rolled away the stone
and were surprised to find a tin king
robust and ready for coronation
and he danced
through all the pain
and pageantry of the people
and reflected back to the world
all of its colour and true light

love is the name
of this leg of the journey
the demons that guard its gate
are formidable indeed
terrible in the mind
unbearable in a warrior's heart

it has been a long dance with our shadows
we've braved each dawn
the biting cold
and let the belle of this isle
distract us with gold and music

but our course is plumb and true
every tribulation of navigation
was selected and tested
and subjected to the scrutiny
of a non-dualistic tribunal

coronation happened in the intersection
of frenchman street and chartres
                    simple as a kiss

then paraded to the river
where we all lay down our burdens
and give our medicine to the people

MAISON POULET

i dreamt you in a flying house
her whirly-gigged blades
disturbed the droning air
as you wrangled the pulleys

you were not alone in there:
the knight of the golden vest opposed you
with machinations of his own
and the people of the village
who came for your demonstration
were well-appointed and wind-blown
as you helicoptered melodiously

there was the accordion player
whom i had followed
across the ocean and up the alps
the dancer who simply felt too much
and the dealers of poisons meant
to enhance the experience
in meticulously casual suits

it was truly a moment of great wonder
and i questioned what it meant
for this hyperpopular ramshackle hamlet
and how long the danger could last
with its tell-tale tapping
of a blade out of balance

these machines we build
are transporting us to destinations
that we forget to demand
before waking

THE PROSTHETIC MIRACLES
OF ST. ROCH

we went to st. roch's to read the bones
and ask questions that almanacs
had no response to

with the gates opened you could finally stand
in the place of the dead
and appreciate the unsugared finery
of a barbaric centurion

an older, wiser altar boy
was appointed as our guide
his fingerprints worn smooth
by the soft, red bricks

he was not the usual sort of guide;
pontificating facts and pimping legends
he just left us alone
and went off to caress the stones

they say that deadmen tell no tales
but you know in new orleans that ain't true
all they do, sun-up to sundown
is chatter: if anyone comes to sit a spell
they get an awful earful

and the only problem i got with the dead
is that they're a bit obsessed with the past:
it is a very circuitous path
getting around to the subject of future

but they do know, reminds the altarboy
in their scatterbrain way
they keep the prosthetics there as
encouragement:
your miracle is due.

so if you go to the cemetery
carry patience in your heart
remember that time is different
when you're stacked six generations deep
and pay regards to the gatekeep

you're sure to meet him again one day

COYOTE AND WHITE CRANE

it would not be the first time the puppeteers
had employed a brown face
to do their dirty work
        gutting the public trust
whilst in the desert, a new islamic state
has recruits from normandy and great britain
swinging severe swords
against their own oppressive culture
attempting to decapitate
the white man's burden

i met an american sniper
before my job in the forest began
he was of the modoc clan
riddled with res' scars
he handed me a service knife
asking me to cut him

it was my road partner who did the job.
while i pressure-wrapped the arterial jet
white crane dipped two fingers
and dressed my cheeks in his blood
declaring he would take from me
a gilly: a snatch of camouflage
the last of my service issue
he would rob me of my burden

and to my heart i would take his.
what this country and white skin
has taken from his land and people

coyote watched curiously
on the other side of the tracks
these lunatics, the two-leggeds
confusing identities
swapping skins

LUNCH WITH THE BARONESS
DE PONTALBA

she skipped her yoga class
because she was hungry
and there was something she had to ask me

she does not order the shrimp remoulade
stuffed avocado nor the fish steak
even the baroness must pay for such things

what she does order
waits on the plate
has grown cold with the telling
of an interminable back story
that doesn't articulate the question
so i must be firm but nurturing
and its funny, but for now
i even like the neurosis

she heeds the call for silence, and eats
falls into the bread and the meats
with a gratitude and relief
of one who has been in flight
from some faceless thief

i am not used
to being the stable boy
but this racehorse, proud
            and high-strung
is true to herself, at least

and i am a lover of the beauty
                and peace
that enters the emperor's courtyard
when the baroness stills her quivering flanks

REGAIN THE SILENCE

time gets lost
amongst star-crossed lovers
shim-sham brothers
the consumptive hustle
feeding our demons

so i make an example
step into a temple
honor agreements
whatever the cost to my knees
i kneel

simple chimes ring
in the breeze that tumbles through
open air markets
raised *lanna* houses
buddha-tree gardens
and between you, and me

explaining in plain language
the message
that never makes it to the tongue

it is almost sunset and the bells have rung
scooters buzz angry, over-fed thoughts
towards what we have lost

i remember the stars, and the silence
i remember simplicity
not feeling the need to buy
one single thing
when all i needed came from the earth

i remember my animal births
when i stare at stone dragons and elephant *stupas*
guarding one hair's-breadth of relic
and regain the silence
as i wander alone, comprehending
my own alien cosmos

time comes untangled, and drops
from the stars
that shine from the roof of the temple

SECONDLINE
for dinerral shavers

i am waiting

in the cracked street
sinking into the asphalt
like the broken houses
all around
and the faces in this tableau
are a million shades of coffee
all streaked with tears

i am growing roots here
the mist is fine and pulls us
        a little further down
a trumpet barks impatiently;
but the preacher still rumbles
behind red bricks

it is electric out here
where tragedy upon tragedy
is spread out in blue sheets
nailed to the rooftops
all eyes are on the door

        the trumpet bleats
        a last complaint
        causes a white dove
        to materialize there

and he is announced!
his mourners are screaming
the only song appropriate
to strike courage into the band

and his casket rolls out
on waves of gold
tones before open throats
raised hands
here is another of our own
passing in the street before us

see the story of his life
dancing all around you
from the house where he was born
through the empty projects
through his tragedies and victories

and hear it
in the beat of some kid
who magically, just for today
hits that snaredrum
just like him

and follow it
unto his final rest
and dance out as much of his mourning
as you can today
because, brothers and sisters
     another secondline
     is on the way

SOBRIETY'S ANXIETIES

the passion of the manic state
is unsustainable: burned body
broken-down relationships
intoxicated vision. the derivation
of all these poetic inspirations
my mad moon insinuations
now suddenly abate?
is this the onset of wisdom?

what cruel trick of fate!
i have taken up yoga and meditation
it is painful and awkward
you may run, but not escape soon
the conditioning of rustbucket taprooms
the better part of your relations
are grunt dragoons; the rank and file

you were born a jack
and yearned to hack
at the roots of the poetry
what's that say for wisdom?

to poison marry production
discipline. construction.
routine and order
make yourself some borders
that was the plan
but where has all the passion gone?

i only know to keep working in the dark
to eat hard tack and pray that god will notice
set fire to the moon again

TAKES A DUMMY TO KNOW

two sips into an americano, and
the pope of fat city drops, sweating
into the nearest chair; apoplectic
his alb askance, the st. vitus dance
manifests as glossalalia, the gift of gab
swears he's wise to the game
but he don't know the score

fifteen minutes later sees
his holiness
skating round the corner, after
twenty bucks of high intent
dusting a retinue of dirty pilgrims
                              in his wake

it's an infallible doctrine
from the holy see of shiftless grace
when he comes back, you can see by his face
that he's now so high he's *under* the bottom
knowing he cannot get lower, he cannot fall

i feel like i've seen giants walking
behind those old-world eyes
the scent of doom detected
in that flaring roman nose

these new orleans sicilians
are a force of nature
they do that shit so you don't have to

i seen two-finger johnnie take enough pills
to win a race in metairie
come back to decatur street
singin' like sinatra

come back, in fact
with the keys to shangri-la
martyrs and wise guys, every one of them
but they don't know the score

THE MULE TRADE

desperate nights on jackson square
where survival will drive you to daft derision
our animal waits with a passing grace
for the wealth of nation's
hee-haw decision

there's dung in the diapers
wedding guests come flocking round
we hawk but get no takers
for a pittance and the right to work
we're made subject
to thugs and fakers

but amidst this, too
cathedral bells
and peals of innocent laughter
parades of people when the games let out
and a sun gone gold on a city
now three hundred years old

you can hear us out there
hawking wares of education
and transportation
history and architecture
epidemics and floods
battles and betrayals
death comes in many costumes
and then after death, in the darkest hour
we sell sordid tales under our breath
before hustling the mules
back to the stables

WOLFSBANE

i pinned your likeness
to the processional altar
smirking skull
broken fleur-de-lys
i had for sometime suspected
that you had murdered your brother
that we had been feeding the wrong wolf

we found the root of your vine
entwined with the spine
down the sacral tailbone
how you writhed
and roared when we pulled you

we named you
and sent you back out in the night

i don't really mean to blame you
i made the choices which invited you in
i've been a long time running
under a shattered moon

we've shared this body for decades
but you're a curse on my relations
and i can no longer shelter your shade
              i am turning to the light

away from the cross, the place of skulls
away from the kiss of your betrayal
on all soul's day, we walked you down the levee
me and the skeleton woman
hand in bony hand

and waited as they consigned
your body to the flame
the dead pulling you into their migration

our big ship
has finally weighed anchor
and sailed off the chain

HOME AFTER THE MISSED DISASTER

this storm was book-ended by rainbows
jeremy said; southern decadence
but i remembered the people's covenants

if you can reckon the blessings of a city
        gone soft
silent as a shadow
the moon cast aloft
lending tender lightness
to the breeze at night
the streets are mostly empty
gliding on my bike
and all my lovely neighbors
grilling out or gathered round
a single flame or on the ground
spilling into the barfront sidewalks
calling my name. unashamed
craving a face they know just a enough
to trust, after things had looked so black

the silent city stretches for miles
down darkened streets both smooth and rough
a few downed lines
she smells of swamp
the not-distant gulf
full of cypress seeds and oak leaves

a well-placed generator lends its light
to the one-night jazz joint
and we've gone back in time
some magic charm is upon us;
we escaped the power grid

dreams we had of beatnick life
are alive tonight, right here; the spark
spirits the trumpet's mainline
young ladies in their negligeés
swing right in time
sippin' cocktails, they feel no pain

i keep cruising past saturn
dj mattie smiles and winks
to the night rider gliding silent by
quietly counting the gentle blessings
in the wake of an almost-hurricane

LIVING THE CLICHÉ

i should by now be well beyond this
shabby hand-me-down glamour
the pall mall raspy singer
the chintzy electric piano
red lights and lukewarm beer

i keep comin' in here to roll the bones
to cruise the dames
to taste the old world
before it's all bought up
by the corporate profane

i'm waiting for my life to arrive
here on the isle of broken toys
we are all more or less
here for the same damn thing

for some, it's just a stop off
or a jumping-off place
but for me it seems to be
the highest rung that i can ring

the root doctor himself
sat on this very spot
saw heaven's door
tilted back on his barstool
and like that, was no more

it's a path with heart, but i wonder:
if it's mine
and do i really want to be a fancy fixture
in some well-appointed hell?

HOMETOWN HAINTS

this little brokewing oriole
come flyin in here, a jailbird
most likely from dundalk, or edgemere
mobtown toughs
broken knuckle boxing buffs
got ways to hide their spiritual side
prison tats
no time for that
getting-to-know-you business

beware the handshake that conceals a snake
down here by the mission
all saints know how to shuck oysters
jive, spange a five
stay alive.

they say the veil is lifted tonight
so we raise a ruckus
feed the dead and hold the salt
our stories are full of laughter

when you're in the everafter
the one thing you don't miss is the tears
of grief. so we gather
urban shamans, streetwise haints
and young turk pugilists
to light the candles
remember our dead
stand and deliver with that black band
at your side
no way to hide the spiritual on this night
all saints rise up
daredevil lights in the sky

come together
feast the ancestors
wipe those saltwater tears from your eyes

WE GOT THIS DAY

for champ, supersunday 2017

we got this day
to give thanks
to dance it out natural
in the street
we come for that royal taste
to laugh and cry and rage and sing
our holy song
this, the way we say
i dig. i get you, god.
i take what you got to give

blow them trombones
we gonna get there, i swear
each one's got their own life to live
so eat some crawfish, drink some beer
...we gonna let it all go clear

maybe the earth *is* dirty
maybe the flesh corrupts
i can't hold nothin' back no-more
it's time to let love in

come dance with me, now
all the way to the door
we 'bout to break off the hinges

all i really care about
is to be able to say
that when i was there
i was fully there
            all the way
and when it's time to go

i do it with pride;
i do it with love.

today
is an exceptional day

THROWN BONES

runic letters in the embers
a beach fire forged from the sky-clad lake
swathed in clouds that scrape the ground
and the stone silence that accompanies us
through every stage of our intimacy

in there is a granite mass
i have not cracked
nor do i dare

vulnerability calls to responsibility
to care, though this leg of the trip
is fraught with lessons of impermanence
the dog has tried to drown himself twice
i can only hold space and wait; learn

to have without holding
to touch without owning
a higher purpose in our wanting
divine design within the dalliance

there are barbs within the sweetness
translucent spines line love's flesh
throw the bones into the fire
read the sigils burning
in the silence, divine
a hard-won learning

THE HOLY BOAT

snug in her slip, the little ship
is lively on intelligent waters
just a bit of elemental magic
shifts us from sunset to eternal dawn

we made it through the windy night
light is breaking after the storm
and we are thankful for the wash
which sent us to shelter together
for a few quiet hours below decks

giving breath to what is true, despite
the flux of weather and tide
we're quick-tethered to the dock
but the ship is always in motion

and we laughed aloud at the thought
of the effort of every raindrop
to retain its individuality
upon kissing mother ocean

we bless even the resistance
to this eventuality
the water learns happy secrets
as they dribble from our hearts
and go splashing out the scuppers

in this instance
the ship's a temple
and all the sailors are holy lovers

THE KNICKERBOCKER
for Sascha DuBrul

riding north; the knickerbocker
a rocker on the rails
smooth sailing
out upon the sunny hudson
again enroute to rendezvous with you, old
    friend
my rootstock, my seed-gatherer; your
crazywise eyes, barrelchested hugs
the shock of your hair
still punk rock after all these years
to see you here in the functioning land
to feel your hand on my shoulder
though we're getting older
we remember the smell of madness
together and apart
to still be alive and still have hearts
which beat fierce
and true to the wild
spirits which drove us out and beyond
in the first place
to have guardians of the memory
of our former faces
this is the treasure which cannot find its
    measure
in our current currencies

the economies of making a killin'
might work for them white collar villians
but we came here to make a livin'

so rosin the bow and wash off the hoe
cuz its farmer's night at the pub

and the kids clean up real nice
so as to rub elbows with the old guys
while the grub keeps getting better
and we now talk more about the weather
than any semantics of our anarchy

and when i think of all the antics
we perpetrated on unsuspecting society
i gotta laugh, gotta holler
hooray for the riff-raff
i hope all the new blackcollars learn
to sing along, cuz its a long song
and if you want to stay strong
it takes a sense of humour

i think i can safely say that
we made it to this day because
we were interested in much more than survival

so many of our people never make this
arrival
go insane or fall off the train
before it ever pulls into station

we know our destination
is and will still be
a little further down the road, so
what will we say to these
greenhaired youngbloods
treadin' in our old tracks, other than
to make them deep and clear enough
that they're intrigued to follow?
even st. ignatius grew sagacious
by the artful mimicry of holy heroes

so do you suppose as this knickerbocker
expresses by steam and whistles that
it's ready again to be underway
we can hope for tomorrow's seeds
to sprout
in these
our fertile valleys?

DREAMING IN THE BONE BOAT

three dangers you must pass:
over mountain borders
mired in despair
then lost and remembering
nothing but your dreams

the goddess will manifest
in anything that looks like love.
the lover won't even know

this power birthing in her;
a natural cycle
you may rest in the certainty
that there is no escape
you swim hard
you leap
you change shape: no matter

she has cast wide her nets
while the ocean grows ever smaller

the skeleton woman comes close
to drink your earnest and heartfelt tears

she will never question why she loves you

THE NIGHT OF ENTWINED DRAGONS

tailbone taproot in the sand
grown down and loosed upon the prey
on the quest, sunset and
moonrise upon the sound before me
trainsong barreling through
the woods at my back

an original howling
star message
too sad to translate
body shock. misanthropy
run to rock, to sea
rootshadow
under the tree
where policeman's light cannot find me

i am the rock
be the rock
i love the rock
i bring the rock and the rock brings me
through petroglyph myth and eventually
they call off the search

officers of the peace have to sleep sometime
        not wolf
        not moon
breaking madly through the trees
awakens a family of racoons
bumbling tumblers cooing chatter
bold enough to touch a saint

everything's gone silent now
a clean vessel, to let the moonlight in
two golden dragons
        making love between the shores
silent ferry pouring light
        upon the mystic sound
original howling, self-knowing
this is my holy grail
this moment. always here
        waiting for us all

from birth to death, make friends
with the universe

now i'm a holy arrow
pointed at the bloody moon
draining slowly into the sound
a howling. a knowing
and home again as the dawn is showing

GNASH

it may be from you
where i first learned to bite
when you came drunk to me
in the middle of the night

the moon shone crazy
through the broken window pane
the witch said you were lazy
and took us both for punishment

the backwards clock
the twisted stairs
the house that moaned
the ghost that cared

none of these horrors could compare
to the thing that compelled you:
the real nightmare

and now you are where?
not in that hospital bed
not in those tubes
not in the will of the physicians
who have thus far refused
your orders not to resuscitate

i haven't done it, yet
gone all the way in
met you in meditation
asked where you have been

and where do you want to go?
is there something here you still want to do?
the next life must be attempted with this one
giving up is not an option
you just prolong your time in hell

i stand in the half-moon light
and gnash my jagged teeth
and this is what you've left me with
the heritage, the legacy

i wish that we were wolves
so that i could bite your throat
so tenderly, old one
and tell you now it's time
for the cub to be the one in charge
and to bring you meat from the kill
and let your light burn down

but this life did not grant us
an ending so neat
so i bite down.
i gnash my teeth.

THE WAY THROUGH

city park protest / may 2015

i'm trying to learn how to love everyone
perceive our places in the mandala
here where we are gathered
in supposed opposition

when you don't know what to do
it is advisable to be still
this way the genius of the present moment
can make its way through

despite fences and police and protest radio
it is the same beast
and the same chance to release it

in fact, not knowing
may be part of the answer

the ant's response is to keep working
only bite in defense
or if there's a chance at food

here where i sit
i am both a problem and an opportunity
perfectly responded to
with the self-same pincers

IN TOWNS WHERE THEY STILL KNOW EACH OTHER

we've been stretched so thin
on miracle products
big box religion
patriot games and credit card sin

there's a decades-old air of desperation
in our money
made of tin
swaddle your babes in robot distractions
never let the fresh air in

but its not yet all gone to ruin
there remain a few forests
some waters seem pure
there are folks who live
with hearts crazed and wild-open

in derelict mining towns
on silent darkened streets
you and i go to find them
to sing of airs we found in forests
in high desert or out to sea
in the towns where they still know each other
not afraid to play or sing

simple agents of inspiration
invoke anew an age-old dream
of a country built on equal measure
where you can give a damn
and still stand free
not based on enterprise, nor regulation
but a grace born of diversity

you and i will go amongst them
with our innocent faith in liberty
our savage hearts will call the others
in forests and towns and down to the sea

SLIPPING THE PERFECT GIG-LINE

i am slowly building
a daytime countenance
often fractured and restored
a perfect gig-line
medals and bars; a spitshine
my stripes: a crafted air of purpose
the regulations and compliances
unheard of from pack-less alphas
but lean times do make us crafty

night time i slip
'neath chainlink wattles
to the fens and more brackish values
coyote-rich with the slender brothers
and rangy sisters skulking about
in the shadows
they see you coming and know
you'll say one thing and do the other

until you're back in your dirt church
the mother den
where each pretense is a promise
where craftiness and self-defense
are the noble tools of the trade

in the shade i yowl
i whip and flail
shaking off the straightjacket curse
begging the bone bride for freedom

and once the false skin is stripped
i sleep awhile upon the earth
dead to the world before an open crypt

death holds no power over me
i have dug no graves, no furrows plowed
neither spilt nor swallowed seeds

when the moon rises:
an irish goodbye
forgive my impetuous sprint
collars and conventions are not for me
and i have all the daytime lent

what little discipline i have
to the mask of humans and their petty woes
so when the *chasse gallerie* calls me anon
one quick kiss and then
release, i go

to a liminal dance amongst the faeries
before returning to the daytime countenance

THE PUNCTUAL

clocked. pegged.
riven to a rhythm
a trajectory. *logos:*
apollo's arias of simple lines
straight time.
> the myth
> the passion
> minimalism

as the bullet flies
the apparent absence of improvisation
grid-locked.
clocked.

this poem wants to fit in a box
> on the scale
ten pairs of clean, white socks
> a new razor

barbasol
> and not a cloud in the sky
29 minutes walk along the docks
> an icy calculation
> > clocked.

> americano.
> espresso.

the fox speaks
in terse confessions of text

> what happens next; i don't know
i'm too pressed for speculation
i'm clocked.

> it's time to go

THE MAN IN THE BLACK HAT

the old man is keeping his watch
from beneath the brim
of a tattered black top-hat

reptile the eyes
false the smile
in truth, he is grim
a shrewd huckster
a lewd angel
a trickster
keeping tabs on the quarter rat youngsters

a black-clad gator
an old-goat satyr
waiting for the doldrums of summer
to strike

i have curbed my darkness
and fallen prey again
the siren song of vampires
keeps me up all night

i have seen him at his breakfast
when i'm shaking off the tremors
nocturnal ramblings still
rumbling 'neath the surface

he is a daytime purveyor of dream
in the city that forgot to sleep
i am crawling through the quarter
in search of my own shadow

silent lest the gator keep
score on my nocturnal indulgence

NOW START AGAIN

in *lahu* village
i am up before the sun
before the teacher, before the self
the villagers, *farang*

i am alone on the mountain platform
to swallow this sliver of moon
      it is not meditation
      it is worship.
now i have to start again

in *lahu* village, i am quiet
      i am distant
my heart is with the dogs, howling
while the mayor of the coconut bar
barks out today's announcements
                a-hep!

in *lahu* village i sit on the mat
i am no longer hands, nor the back
receiving this technique
i am the one who swallowed the moon
the dreamer awake behind the dream

in *lahu* village there is a man
with only three teeth, who plucks
a pretty mean thai banjo blues

for three thousand year, only one song:
papaya-banana-cooking! no problem!

beyond that
we understand each other like quiet men

now start again

FLY ON HOME
katrina evacuation, NYC

we got out by walking on water
staying light, taking time to stretch
                              to breathe
keeping in mind
the permanent permeations of magic

after running all day
we lay trusting
on the soft belly of earth
and cried a little
beneath alabama stars

since then it's been a constant contact
a handhold
nature's sing-song rhythms
rocking us into a longhaul tempo

we, without destinations
find ourselves in synchronistic co-ordinates
and have time to hear the humming of ley-lines
whence we draw strength
for the indefinite road ahead

she awoke, as usual
a little later than me
she yawned, scratched her mane
and shook loose what i first mistook
for a multicoloured cape
which turned out to be wet wings
still sticky from the chrysalis
and i thought, my god
i'll never keep up with beauty

but then she slipped a slender arm
around my back and pulled
one black raven feather;
my very own wings.
quivering
waking
singing to be skyborne

we sat on a manhattan rooftop
just smoking
watching colour well up from the city
letting our wings dry
until that last slip of sunset orange
caught fire and buried itself in her hair

c'mon, she said
they're ready. let's fly on home

but where is that *now*, i wondered

she pointed to the night, the waning moon:
we may land from time to time, said she
but home
is wherever we can be free

ROOTFIRE

who do you think it is, hollering
'bout those kids on the corner?
going at it, doing their thing
busting through
the dirty concrete

these roots are unstoppable
have toppled great houses before
empires built on selling their bodies
have been torn asunder, no wonder:
rootwork
is not a thing to be trifled with

that bass drum is a cannon
it's a revolution
burning up the atlantic ocean
there are still fires burning down in haiti
des feux lá-bas en saint domingue

and we thank that fire for keeping us warm
for heating up this jailhouse rock
for keeping the yanks on constant alarm
it rises in ranks with every black shot
for some, this fire
is the only one they got

so give your everything
torpedoes and tourists be damned
pay no mind to the frenchmen street cops:
do your thing

this is your shot.

ISLEÑO LULLABY

¿qué es esto; el jaillo?
lo que nos tráe aún más
al borde del mar
desde la orilla conocida
hacía un mundo nuevo

here am i in the new world
awaiting the flowering
of human consciousness
i find it in very tiny things
very specific and tactile things
the piercing of pages in a handbound book
the minute embellishments that belie
the clarinetist's love for his work

él sólo querría darme luz

in little couplets of forgetting
knowing i can take all this in
here am i again
in my adopted *país*
the only snailshell i've ever known
curled inside a golden ratio
if there be any rationale for this

to me, it is like the *fado*
the strange stigmata
de la guitarra portugesa
even more than these comic *décimas*
el grito gitano
the alto soprano
ah-ro-ro
if my child would sleep

i would give him this *regalo:*
      el jaillo
that which most pulls us back
to the edge of the sea,
the world that we know

PRESENCE IN THE STRIKE

the hawk, in its sharp ascent
revels in that weightless moment
when up and down no longer have meaning
                the diver down
                ensorcelled by the shimmering blues
that moment in the meditation
when you push through your impermanence
and no longer want to come back
to the elaborate fiction
you've bound yourself to

if you could turn in any direction
you would head straight back to the source
but you don't know where that is anymore

while the slow, precise path you're upon
is sinuous, serendipitous
leading you down to your lay-low place
spitting coffin nails all the way

facing mortality on this sober morn
i would like to think i'm brave, but
the chickens and me all agree
that none of us gets out of this alive

one life
one pass of the samurai blade
where to strike?
when?

THE SHINING VISION

from this height above the clouds
i can see the shining
monasteries of lhasa
though they exist on the other side
of the world.

experiencing the cycle of darkness
one wonders at the journey
that people have taken
to acquire such dire wisdom

now we live in a world
that has lost sight of such a vision
and one must wonder
if things will continue to deteriorate

except, in my personal experience
life continues to improve

i am descending through the clouds, now
the golden light of morning throws
shadows behind me like
frightened wraiths
illuminates
the mighty forests of cypress
upon lake ponchartrain
the tankers on the mississippi
and even the petroleum plant
sprawled by the river

i am going to touch the ground in my city
and it will be my work
to continue to see this shining vision

THE GARDENER'S PRAYER

they call this a wildcraft
what we've turned our hands to
in these endangered lands
we make our stand
where love is an indigenous species
slow down. try to understand
the whispers in the seed bed
the harmony of this garden
how we nurture and are nurtured by
how we unite ourselves to what's grown

without trying to own.
there is a sacred design here
our roots have intertwined and spread
into rhizomatic relationships
the green spark of love bursting upwards
in a virgin forest of fellow dreamers

we have to learn to hold hands
we cannot help but impact one another
the long lineage
that we belong to
and are taking from
and are adding to
is the song of gardeners who've come before

the medicine wheel. come and kneel
let our work be a prayer
let the fruit of what we grow here
be food to our souls
food to all the souls
who lend hands tending to this holy work

there is a sacred design here
it falls to us
to steward this love
in the sanctuary of the wild
to honor relations by tending the garden

THE CEREMONY OF NIGHT

it was night
and a spirit had come upon us

i took you to a churchyard
the old *place d'armes*
a good drop-off point
                for wayward skeletons

i just got back in town
and already it's got its hooks in me
every exchange we made
opened hearts and made us wealthy

you, with your imaginary close-up
and me, turning the city into a poem
why else have we been given
these nights of may?

to hawk over our escapades?
to send our dream-selves soaring?
over slate rooftops
to record our urchin lives
with dragonfly's eyes

we float onto the ceremony
of coyote grifters
scumbags and tourists
the hardened locals in their cups
past the vampire bars, idle buskers
become occasional angels of mercy

sometimes a gift of tobacco engenders
a proffering of prophecy
sometimes we become our own enemies
and wake up sunnyside anyway

who's gonna say no to love?
somebody does, but not me
not tonight

i've yet to hit too much

THE DANGER ANGELS

the danger angels are descending
torn wings ever blacker
in the smog-grey morn

inhabiting the clothes
of our sad-eyed friends
they have trafficked with dark souls
in dark dens.
a foot in the bright,
a foot in the shade
they ply the trade of gentle extraction
for souls
in immortal danger
pull you
from auto-centric gulags
without crushing the precious spirit

the danger angels know the night
and all its labyrinthine ways
the lower quarter, the coke joints
black leather and blood

roughnecked bodhisattvas
metaphysical pararescues
whose tarnished haloes glint
when daylight slots like blades
through the gates of the abbey

as they walk home one more
drunken refugee

THE WILL TO CHANGE

if we all pull together
on something besides the nightly till
we could tilt the world
throw this axis of evil into a wobble

we are the progenitors
of everything we could do without
                don't worry about it;
i'm elbow-tight right beside you
mired in the filth and the muck

what dreams do you hold allegiance to?
what bright eagle turned west
as soon as you loosed your bow?

this place is full of prospectors
and god is laughing at us all
the mirth, i suppose
is due to a lack of will to change

nothing is inevitable
but the steady tide of erosion
puts us in a sort of paralysis

shake the pan for a little gold
the road is paved with such intentions

HALO

two can be as one:
my thoughts flowed out
to the place where you'd been backlit
by the sun. the cold had been driven
a little further off by your nearness, and
bright adherence to the selective notion
of what it means to be primary

i am a fool to let such things pass
or any promissory notes at all
when i can't play a single scale

noise is what i know
i push through my tongue-tied past
to find what truly needs to be said
and someday i will set a schedule
to sing at the same time daily
diurnal disciplines not deviated
by all my nightly yowling

but i am going to need a whole chicken
before i get to that party
i can tell some wolfy jams
are gonna be goin' down

you had difficult dreams, then
with the sun
perambulating your head

COMMUNITY AGRICULTURE

relieved from duty finds me
with tools in the hand and
a bead upon the brow

what rest knows a punk
born to the brawn of service?
but this, too: a sort of heaven
the *shambhala* of communal toil

ego it may be;
or folly
or addiction to scratch the calluses
green trees and blue skies
the hopeful allure of black soil
fresh-turned in the sun
brings these bodies as one
to sing the praises of the land's abundance

nor will we shirk
our turn at the stove
we will feed and in turn be fed

labour is my gift
born of love, not coercion
i'll take my vacation days
when i'm gone and dead

MARDI GRAS RAVEN
ash wednesday 2006

the raven came upon me
in full regalia
black ink dripping
from the tips of his wings

came swooping into the parade
singing omens
dropping scrolls
and death walked close behind

we were in the middle of forgetting
swimming through the drunken streets
when the mardi gras raven
cawed us awake
a cacophony of colours spilled
from that house on clouet street

with our numbers swelled
by the recently departed
the society of st. anne stepped gaily forth
to perform the solemn duty of debauchery
last rites
for a thing called justice

there were moments when i was airborne
soaring over the brassband
to lay down our burden by the riverside

every step of our fevered dancing was met
by denizens from down below
and every spilled drop was drunk
                    by martyred spirits

and i cried beneath the snapping ribbons
stepping out into the waters:
funeral-baptism for one caught between worlds
        ...til the black bird cawed me back

messenger
always brings bad news
signs squared against one another
but it is in these travails
which spring from the midst of our revelry
whence we find strength
for the long road ahead

they are the diamond threads that we use
to stitch together the great human family
the living
and the dead

the raven came to wake me up
before even the bone crews
could rattle me from dreams

DANCING TO THE GATES
for siddhartha

let me take your weight
on my shoulders, hold you
fast about my neck
cradle you like blood kin
as you melt into my chest

for showing me the inner wild
illuminating the cosmic ties
my packmate, my grandfather child
my teenage elder, roadbrother defender
we will stare like this, into the lens
our bond frozen-snared, the camera
captures the care
before our ship's forever wrecked

this is how i'll hold you
even when i'm letting go
over and again into the river
an endless flow beyond these shores

this is for the howl
that you have loosed into the heavens
for the hardships you withstood
for the nights that you stood guard
when we were banished to the woods
for every holy mile we pilgrimaged together

i'll shoulder this painful burden
loving what i know i'll lose
committing myself completely
to the steps of our warrior dance

and i'll dance you to the gates, my brother
will you wait for me on the other side?

REBUILDING

raise your glass
to the city of the past:
what has been can be again

buy me another drink
before the end of the night
we will set right
this house of cards
horses and swords and cups, oh my

the disaster has to return us
to days of simplicity
it seems, but not really
the dealer doles out
new-shattered fractal layers
to keep us on our tipsy toes

an illusion, a cheat
we don't get to play our hand over
but we can lay out the cards
exactly as they were
(according to the historic committee)
and fake it

then pour the first sip on the ground
and leave the last in the cup
for the city that we lost
and the one that's yet to be re-built
are both thirsty for your consideration

THE SUCHNESS OF MIGRATION

in the periphery of this silver dawn
a stray thought
escapes west
as a honking goose
out over the chilly hudson

i bring my breath
back to the edge of the dock
where my efforts are best employed
in nothingness;
apparently at rest

yet i am fully aware of my striving

I WANT TO MAKE LOVE TO YOU

i want to make love to you
i want to rest the four mounds of my fingertips
between your breasts; over your heart
and watch your eyes grow sharp
as you feel the new movement within

i want to smell your skin
under your arms
on the backs of your calves
blending with the fragrance of ferns

i want you to feel me yearn
even if it's only so
that one human, in one world entire
can understand me
the tragic passion, and ardent ferocity
which threaten to tear out of me
like a giant, ripping
his guts from the center of earth

i want to make love to you
to kiss your earlobe
with just the very tip of my tongue
the tiny lips that live there, and send
spiraling gibbous ribbons of night
questing through your blood
in search of nether chakras

i want to make love to you
and forget to breathe
and growl
and let the wolf come
bounding
into the front yard of my mind

i want to make love to you and feel
the strength of my body
lifting you
in easy, dancing waves

i want to make love to you
like a sacred temple harp
running roughened hands
over the arc of our covenant
coaxing moans from the groaning bedsprings
virtuoso duet in our little unsanctioned
        symphony

i want to make love to you, and send
care packages of life juice
to 99 forgotten goddesses

i want to make love to you and repair the tear
in the holy fabric of lust
i want to make love to you and watch
the scars that we've gathered
as our harvest in this unjust world
heal and vanish
before our unblinking eyes
i want to make love to you
and silence the whispering voices
for a few golden hours

i want to make love to you like a holy fire
i want to make love to you with religious
        thirst
i want to make love to you and

                burst

into tears, and sob
and fall asleep on your chest

like a child, who has never known
sorrow, or hunger, or fear

      only safety
and the fullness
of a mindless peace
      and rest

FLOOD STREET
for herbert kearney

these graveyard streets are shifting
back and forth: from the living
to the dead
and i clearly remember what you said
when we came home
to do the work

when you staked your bad boy reputation
to help this poet find shelter
        (as you had for a host of us)
i said, home is a concept
for the metaphysically displaced

i still taste
those bitter herbs
crucified in holy cross
still running blind for love
from the river towards the lake
on flood street

WHIPPOORWILL

it is neither clinical nor cynical
to assert that love
is a migratory whippoorwill
a travelling salesman
a fly-by-night journeyman
a mecca-less pilgrim
a come-back comet
       and out the door again

or cruising by on a slender steed
a beat-up ten-speed
a runner in the marathon
that never ends

when her boat lands upon your shore
when love raps minutely on your midnight door
              open; within
and give no thought for what can be held
can be lost again

whatever the price
love can pay the cost
and love will just as quickly fly away
at least in form
but the feeling will stay
if you don't bother trying to control her

let the songbird land where she will
when dawn breaks, you may find her still
light on your branches
singing the world into being

SUGARSKULL COMPLICITY

everything we used to know about this work
                        has suddenly ebbed
leaving us a quiet sadness
                        a real need to be held
a disturbing and foreboding premonition
that this weather might be bigger and badder
than any of our individual grievances

this whole city used to be a temple
now a walking mausoleum
just the other night i marched
with a bone crew army
600 skeletons deep

used to be that death marked the edges
gave meaning, now
death is the meaning

all the things we used to want to be
used to want to do
and the people we wanted to be with
have just become the sugar coating on the
    skull
in our perpetual day of the dead
i'm looking this knucklebone
right in the eye socket
and i know, now
there is only one dance

so even when the ancient voice is upon me
and the bones bow low in veneration
and hurricanes are swirling
towards our merciful annihilation
        i will not be shaken

the dream has lost all glamour
the spider web has broken
its gossamer gone to grey

i have become one
with the destroyer

THE CONE OF PROBABILITY
27aug12

it's in the atmosphere.
gathering.
a shroud; a cycle.
wind and rain out over the water
barely a thought for the *bon-vivants*
still, at ease in their wine-filled cups

a summer night, and jazz outdoors
the balm that quiets
the fears that could bring
this hurricane upon us

secretly, we telephone
our relatives
the back-up plans
we must avert disaster, again
but we return to the back-yard bacchanalia
jazz swinging into the trees
drenching the night in melodies

if it happened, again
the broken homes and floods
the trauma and the grief
we might throw up our hands this time
walk away from difficult love

it is within the cone of probability
but we don't live for that moment;
we live for this one.
we savour the wine
in its cold bottles
sweating deliciously
in the tiki torch light

sway to the music
open your heart to friends
who could end up being lost
in the gathering uncertainty

THE DOWNSHIFT

five thirty in the marigny
evening breeze of piano and calliope
all we ever do is slow down in this town
ambition is sin: *memento mori*
all rush and haste will go to waste
walk slow as you approach the hollow grave

another iced coffee laced with chicory
set a guitar on your knee
the solution to your worry
is some engineered forgetting
we'll sell you a fine bottle
set you up with sweet song

no amount of honking
will make the geese fly any faster, so
     be at peace
with your disaster

THE EGO HUNTERS

we spent all day chasing demons
whether acquired by black magic
or in the wake of past-life transgressions

it was a long day of resolutions
agreeing to let go, to be un-stuck
of the things that we were made of
dispersing notions of yes and no

there are few tools as efficacious as touch
between two bodies
that used to be lovers

now we are ego hunters
lion-tamers
now we wake up to the bright and cold

realizations: the truth
of where our lives stand
in the balance of the years

that light gets in behind the rib cage
to the wounds made long ago
to identity and attachment
painstory: false glory
            dead gods we should have shed
                 left out in the snow
                     buried in the garden

or hung on a post; as warning
this is a dangerous place for ego

RACCOON SARCASM

fear's a killer,
so still your mind
the access point to
the other side

i came for learning
you came for release
our teacher having passed his body of knowledge
dark warriors pressed in close
while rock and roll dragons descended
toward this cut-up patch of the void

people mock and laugh
but it was coming back alive
we dodged thundering airboats and slid
silent swamp ninjas
across the wet din of life

and saw gape-mouthed
the great tourists
huge and money-fat
their open lips flubbered
as they passed us burning gas

we left only quiet eddies
though i own we are not much better
and if the raccoons get their paws
on some paint and brushes
what sort of signs will we be reading?

more garbage, please.

i do not always know the shape that love will take
but i fancy i know how it tastes
and it must be free or it's not love.

the gators remain silent. the hawk and heron
forsake their place at such
blowhard displays
the egrets silent stalk and spear their prey
will turn only one eye in doleful regard
turns out, in fact: it wasn't that hard
a riddle: for they did know
the eclipsing shape of love

THE BEAUTIFUL BONES

and again called to the river bend
with you, who listens
to all the beautiful bones
who counts every rib and vertebra
not yet claimed
by springtime flood, by wake and tide
or the cruel blade of the bush-hog
on the *batture*-side of the *levée*

now who won't let go?
the alter-egos we build
while dropping the lesser blows
of some magnificent story

if we can resist our addiction to definition
resist the urge to *tell* it.
live it.
let the full-being song of the cicadas
rapt in praise of the universe
mellow with the afternoon blues
left from last night's revelry
love's latest casualty
this full-circle reality

these bones still have some poems
send me again to the river bend
to collect them

SUMMERTIME LULL

all the life you could never plan for
 thunderclap synchronicities
 coffeeshop collaborations
our schemes to dodge the deluge
 our dreams do mean something
after all.

every time i think i can sort it out
rhythm comes dripping from the rooftops
rat-a-tat rip-rap playing taps
for the plans you made about today

it is still summer in september.
 surrender
to diluvian detours, determination
to weather other people's trauma drama
dreamless nights, public intoxication
and the silent, insipid mosquitoes' bite
moods inspired by moonrise

why resist?
the crazyquilt collective
conundrum awash
in the languid and the lush
lyric of louisiana's
post-precipitation hush

SMOKING MONK

i am particular to the draft and hew
of this avuncular rebel monk
bamboo-lean and dark with mean
lines of ink from his days as a punk

in this forest retreat
he's renounced all other trappings
but the cool of the street is still on him
see: tong lights a smoke
and the clouds of nirvana
shuffle over his shoulder

brown bean ruddy complexity
i vow: the azimuth i see
makes sense to me
no tea ceremony
just instant coffee

and maybe
that instant of *samadhi* you get
when he smiles and dumps
his round bowl of alms
into your borrowed basket

both of you
bare feet in the street

THE BEAR WITNESS

demonstration of the rising
heat index: body count
the big thaw evident
in the overheating of this polar body

pushed out of her native environment
swimming in strange waters
striving for new tongues
desperate survival of the species
the biological stresses on us all

it remains to be seen
if there is a battle worth winning

where the ice is steadily thinning
and methane bursts from frozen earth
as if to say; here is what you wanted
my children, my final gift

death is common to us all

RECORDKEEPERS

this is the place
where the needle always skips
a hiccup in the song, a scratch
an aberrant groove left one day
in late august; seven years past

for a long time
i couldn't leave town at all
without hearing that tragic ballad
and today we recall the anniversary
with another recalcitrant road trip

but i suppose we are stronger now
with deeper grooves, a heavier stylus
surprising ourselves, we pass through the eye
of the needle, past the faint pop in the song
where it all went wrong
without losing the melancholy melody

the moon sails on
        through a haunted landscape
cypress trees, refineries
the world we live in is so precarious
preyed upon by human arrogance
and self-hatred and gluttony
and whatever comes to us from the sky
the angry ocean
is a natural resolve; a call and response
a predictable turn in the opus

as we hum along our migratory path
        flee and return
                resume the chaos
                        for better or for worse

we are the keepers of this song

THE POWER OF MUSIC

it moves into realms
too finely interlaced
to divine, even
with our royal augury

where it comes from, or where it goes
none of us really knows, but we agree
that music is a spiritual path
supersedes our needs and greed
for entertainment. if high enough
it breeds loyalty, entrainment
to sacred beats, our bodies dance
it sends us into trance

and a quiet querulous tremble
that drives our lower quarters
fires the body's breathing
an evanescent burning
unabashed ambulations ambush
your too-tired-to-care façade
and now you're a voice
in the melodic constellation
and if that saxophone holds sway
then all bets are off
i'll burn two day's pay
chasing that primordial yearning
down decatur street and through the gates of hell

like anyone, i have a predilection
for self-destruction. we are all
to some extent, so many moths
to the flame

so turn it up tonight
let me wear out these shoes
once the ritual's under way
no price is too high to pay

to dance these blues into oblivion

BREAKING AND ENTERING

the moon tried to sneak in my bathroom window
between the razors and the orange pomade
tried to sneak in roses
        and firecrackers, of all things
with a momentous and unjaded heart

she didn't expect the crystal transmission
of her message
to be so well-received. she thought
dancing on the bar would make her a pariah
she was so used to love being a one-way street
a parlour trick
like swallowing lightbulbs in the dark
i heard them tinkling in her belly
heard the commotion in the bathroom

i admit she has dangerous timing
traipsing coastal reaches
whilst the tide is coming in
consuming her taboos in public
befriending the ragged people
even the likes of widdershins wolves
seeking refuge in enemy territory

she didn't know the heart of wolves
how long they tended to love
how they carried their wounds a lifetime
in silence, recording the moon's
                        minutest meanings

i have been here many seasons
the moon, though everchanging in her aspect
is a creature of habit after all

the sea betrays her waking emotion
the unwitting pull of her orbit
even a starfish could tell she'd been drinking

i, too have my cycles
have burst naked through the canopy
love without folly is a suburban enterprise

we are sacred monsters
it is our duty to haunt the wastelands
wage war on safe conventions

the moon is not so foreign to me
we shine with the same perplexing light
glinting off the razors
calling for the blood

--------------end of transmission.

Raymond "Moose" Jackson is a self-taught poet and ex-military Detroit native who found his way to New Orleans in 2003 via squatting, direct activism, and trainhopping. He follows ancient traditions of the poet's role in community as truth-sayer, articulator of a people's vision, and psychopomp. His poetry works to restore the sacred relationship between community and place. His environmental play *Loup Garou* won the Big Easy Award for Best Original Work of 2009. Other works, including *Cry You One (2013-2018)*, have toured domestically and abroad at the cutting edge of ritual, public theater, and activism. He performs regularly with New Orleans's experimental jazz community as an improv poet, resulting in the 2012 documentary *Liquid Land* by Michelle Ettlin. Previous publications include *Loup Garou* (Lavender Ink 2010) and *Return to Yakni Chitto* (University of New Orleans Press 2020). Jackson's work has appeared in *A Howling in the Wires* (Gallatin Press 2007), *Stories That Care Forgot* (Last Gasp 2006), and *BOMB Magazine*.